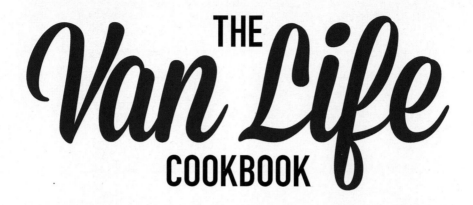

THE Van Life COOKBOOK

THE Van Life COOKBOOK

Delicious Recipes, Simple Techniques, & Easy Meal Prep for the Road Trip Lifestyle

Susan Marque

ULYSSES PRESS

Published by:
ULYSSES PRESS
PO Box 3440
Berkeley, CA 94703
www.ulyssespress.com

ISBN: 978-1-64604-315-6
Library of Congress Control Number: 2021946405

Printed in China
10 9 8 7 6 5 4 3 2 1

Acquisitions editor: Claire Sielaff
Managing editor: Claire Chun
Editor: Kate St.Clair
Proofreader: Michele Anderson
Front cover and interior design: Raquel Castro
Cover photo: © Mr Doomits_ColorEdit/shutterstock.com
Production: Jake Flaherty
Interior photos: shutterstock.com—page 8 © Andrey Armyagov, page 24 © BublikHaus, page 14 © Virrage Images, page 18 © Sergiy Borakovskyy, page 23 © Sushaaa; Adobe Stock—page 13 © Tomasz Zajda, page 21 © Matt

This book is dedicated to Dad, for teaching me to be a resourceful camper, and Mom, for teaching me how to cook.

Contents

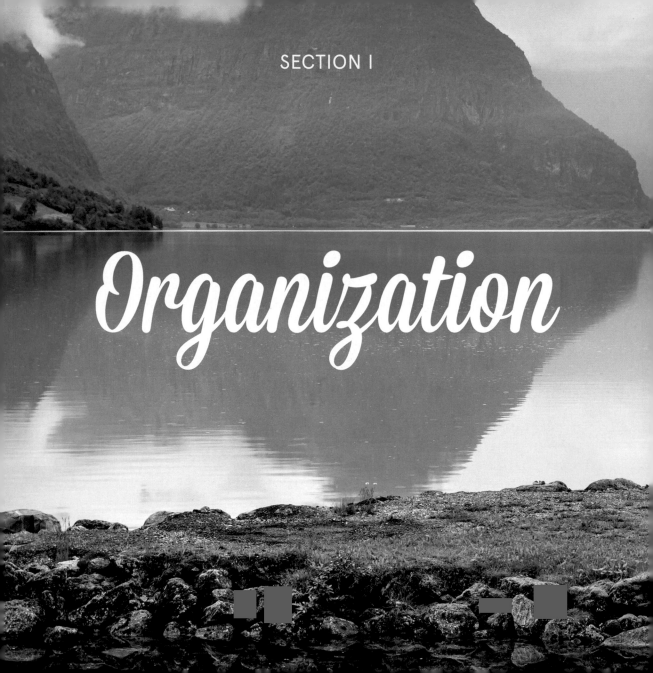

SECTION I

Organization

CHAPTER 1

Introduction

There is something very satisfying about making a good meal. Especially on the road. Maybe it's the fresh air you wake up to, or the free feeling of being mobile or handy. No matter what type of space you have, a large RV, a small camper van, a boat, or a tiny apartment, cooking can be easy and fun.

I once traveled with a boyfriend up the coast of California in a small van without a kitchen. We cooked outside on a grill. Everything tasted *amazing*.

In New York City, I joked that I was camping in the city. I sublet quite a few apartments in the eight years that I lived there. One of my favorites was a tiny space in Tribeca. The owner lived next door and had remodeled the apartments to add extra room to her larger space by slicing off some of the square footage from the studio. As a result, the studio had an under-the-counter fridge in a slender hallway with a counter, sink, and no stove, just a hot plate. When I was looking at the place initially, everyone who knew me said, "No, you can't live there—you cook all your meals." I didn't see a problem. I did buy the smallest toaster oven. (So it wouldn't take up much room on the counter. Every inch counts when you live in close quarters.) I found I could easily cook a three-course meal on that single burner and bake whatever I liked in the teensy oven. Meals didn't always look the same, since I had to use toaster oven pans or whatever I had on the burner. My pizzas and pies were small rectangles instead of round, and my muffins were extra small, but I made some terrific-tasting food.

Most of the time, I cooked a pot of grain in the morning to use all day. Grain won't go bad sitting on the counter for hours. Lunches were often salads I assembled, and dinners were usually cooked in a skillet. I also baked everything from cake to popovers in my tiny oven. That apartment was where I began developing and photographing recipes for publication. It was a doorman elevator building only a couple of blocks from the Hudson River. I found walking through the parks and being near water invigorating, while the city itself was always alive and exciting. I took my lunches up to the rooftop. There were tables and chairs where you could watch all the boats coming and going. Camping comes in many forms.

This cookbook is for anyone who enjoys good food easily made. Many of the recipes are simple to do and won't take much time to execute. Since I am the person making and eating the food, these recipes are geared to my taste, which is, admittedly, not going to be just like yours. That's why they are mostly very flexible. There is nothing wrong with green beans or hot peppers, for example—I simply do not like them. So if they are your favorites, by all means, toss them into things. Many of the recipes are geared so you can add the herbs, spices, and vegetables that appeal to you. That's on purpose—because when you are living in a camper van, you may or may not have access to every type of ingredient all the time. I've included many flexible recipes that you can adjust to what you have on hand, like, or can get.

I've also tried to keep the number of pots and pans to a minimum. It's just more convenient to use less cooking fuel and have less to wash up later. This works well for most situations. If you happen to have more room, or more people, watch the serving amounts and double or triple the recipe as needed.

There are many different situations that coexist with van life cooking. Once you get the hang of making meals in a small kitchen, you may actually find you prefer it. It's a great way to live. One of the key differences, unlike a kitchen in a large house, is that you can usually reach all around your entire cooking area. When you are setting up your camper van space, consider where you'll hang or store wooden spoons, herbs, and spices, as well as small tools, like whisks, measuring cups, and so on. You'll want to be able to grab them without leaving your burner. I've hung things up with hooks, or used small shelves with bungee ties in front of them, so that I can see and access what I need without opening a drawer or digging through other items.

Another thing to consider is where you will hang a couple of kitchen towels. In a large kitchen, towels often go on the oven door handle or on a counter. In a camper van, you might have only a burner and a small sink. I am very fond of large magnetic hooks that I can put up in convenient spots for towels or keys. If you have metal spots, that's an option. You may like hooks with screws or Command strips. Just keep towels handy. Towels are the most-used kitchen item, and if you don't have a place for them, they can end up getting in the way or falling on the floor. Some chefs like to put them in the front of their apron. If you are disciplined enough to always wear an apron, I applaud you. I'm not, but I do keep my cooking tools handy.

Think out your space as much as you can so that it works well for you. And don't get frustrated if you find you need to move items around a little once you really start cooking in your space. That's okay. You might find that

having a cutting board over your sink works well, or you might decide that creating a pull-out cutting board is better. The more comfortable you are with your setup, the easier it will be to create wonderful meals in your camper van, boat, or room.

That also goes for things like knife skills. Do you need to chop a carrot as fast as seasoned chef? No. But getting used to basics, like keeping the tip of your knife on the cutting board as you slice, will make things go faster, smoother, and help you be a happier cook.

I mentioned bungee cords to keep salt, pepper, herbs, and spices on a shelf. You might want to have a different method for holding your jars in place, but remember that a camper van, RV, boat, or any other mobile living space needs to have some way to keep things from falling. If you are

used to having a container near the stove with a bunch of cooking tools and want that in your van life, it's going to have to be secured somehow so that it doesn't end up flying in the air every time you roll over a bump. I like to have my wooden spoons, spatulas, whisks, along with basic herbs and spices visible and easy to access, right near where I'm cooking. It's a lot like an artist having their paint, water, cloth, and brushes near the canvas they are working on. If your space is set up to function well, you'll be a lot happier to be cooking.

Another way to make meals fun, rather than a chore, is to mix things up as much as you can. If you rely too much on the same few meals, you are bound to get bored. Stay inspired. Once you get the hang of cooking in your tiny kitchen, don't stick to five types of stir-fry. Look at food sites or cookbooks once a week and try something new. Stop at a market in your area and pick up a new vegetable or fruit. At the very least, take one of the recipes that you enjoy and just try seasoning it a little differently. The more creative you allow yourself to be, the more fun cooking can be.

When you have limited burners and pans, cook what doesn't need to be as warm first. I usually cook desserts first and let them cool while I cook the main course. Say you are having a soup course and a main course—soups tend to cook quickly and you'll want them hot most of the time. Cook the main course first on the burner and then the soup. Once you get the hang of it, you'll find having limited burners or pans won't really be a problem at all. It might even feel invigorating to think of the meal you want to have, and execute it elegantly, like a well-seasoned chef. Some of the best art is made with constraints. Think of each meal as a fun experiment that you get to eat, or as your artistic creation. The more you enjoy it, the easier it all gets.

CHAPTER 2
Staples and Tools

Staples are the food items that you want to have on hand. Some, such as a good salt, are essential, and I never let myself run out of them. Others, such as pasta, are things I most always have on hand to make a quick meal. You get to choose what the essential things are for you! While I like to buy meat, fish, or poultry directly from a market on the day I'll be making something with them, other people like having canned fish or chicken on their shelf as a staple. I use organic products almost exclusively because they are not only better for us, they taste better too.

Here are a few suggestions for staples I use and the ones that will help you with the recipes in this book.

Salt is essential.

Salt is what makes flavor come alive. You also can't bake without salt, since it is more than a flavor enhancer, it's part of what makes things cook well. Salt's ability to draw out water from vegetables, and help enzymes begin to break down fiber, is one of its magical abilities to transform produce, even without the use of fire. Heat, of course, is transformative and nourishing in its own right, but salt is one staple you can't do without. I have learned over the years that sea salt is tops. Choosing your favorite sea salt will depend on your personal preference. As this is a cookbook and not about individual ingredients, I won't go into all the ways that sea salt is a healthy thing to eat, but there is just nothing like it. While many chefs claim Maldon to be their go-to salt, I lean more toward a nice Italian salt or a *fleur de sel*.

There are three other "salts" that I always have on hand as staples:

- miso paste
- umeboshi (vinegar and pickled plums, or the paste)
- tamari (soy sauce)

Miso paste comes in many varieties. I like having a dark and a lighter miso paste on hand, but if you have space for only one, just choose your favorite. Lighter ones tend to be sweeter, and darker ones tend to be earthier, with a rich umami flavor. They can be used for far more than just miso soup. You can use miso for dressings, sauces, pickling brines, or marinades too.

Umeboshi (ume) may not be something you are used to having around, but it often comes in a small jar and is an ideal ingredient to have for van life because of its versatility and alkalizing ability. Umeboshi has been an Asian staple for thousands of years, and while not well known in the West—yet—I use it all the time in my cooking and whenever I have an upset stomach or feel off. Whole salty-sour plums are potent, so a little goes a long way, but they also add a special flavor that brings out the goodness of other

vegetables. Avocados can go from bland to grand, and a sushi roll will just taste better with a little ume smeared inside.

Umeboshi vinegar is not actually vinegar. It's the brine left over from making the pickles. You can use it in place of vinegar in some dishes, but it also makes a nice salty seasoning for a stir-fry or for a salad dressing. I always have a small bottle on my shelf.

Tamari is usually a soy sauce without additives, and the quality of the salt can be much better than some soy sauces. I prefer it to the lighter shoyu. With tamari, so many things taste good that I end up using it more than the others mentioned. Savory dishes get an extra boost and bland items like tofu easily turn into memorable meals.

After salt, the next staple item needs to be oil.

Fat is the carrier for flavors and is often the medium you cook your food in. While I do water-fry vegetables, or steam them now and again, that's never as satisfying as cooking with oil. Usually a steamed or water-fried item will then be doused with some sort of dressing or sauce that has oil or fat in it. Fat is an essential ingredient in cooking and you will need some type of oil.

Olive oil is my staple of staples in the fat department. An extra-virgin olive oil is versatile and adds a nice flavor. Try to find one that has been pressed recently. Unlike vinegar that might age well, olive oil is really a fruit juice and best when fresh.

Olive oil does not generally work well for baking or high heat. Since you have limited space in a van, you may want to start out with only a good olive oil, or an all-around oil that can take heat well, such as coconut oil, or an organic oil blend such as Nutiva's original organic shortening. I suggest starting out by stocking one oil and then, as you plan meals and progress in your camper van journey, you can add another type of oil.

Vinegar is a staple that I often forget when I move to a new place and am setting up. Vinegar is an ingredient you might use daily in a salad dressing or often in a braised dish. If you don't use it much, it might not be a staple for you, but I find it's worth having a small bottle around to make my dressings, sauces, and pickles.

Other staples are going to be the things you use often. I eat whole grains more than bread so I always have at least a couple on hand, along with dried shiitake mushrooms, and some sort of beans. I start out with a few seasonings and add more when needed. Here's what a sample staple grocery list might look like. Think about what you use most often and want to have on hand in your camper van. Consider what you have room for too.

Sample staple grocery list:

- Extra-virgin olive oil
- Sea salt
- Apple cider vinegar
- Miso paste
- Tamari
- Umeboshi plums
- Brown rice
- Millet
- Organic canned chickpeas
- Small rice wraps
- Sushi nori
- Flour
- Pasta

A note on flour: Many staple ingredients can last for a long time and still be good—flour is not one. Flour is a whole grain that has been ground very fine. As soon as whole grains are ground, they oxidize. Oxidation ages them very quickly. This creates rancid flour, which is often used anyway—I don't recommend it. You will know the flour you have is rancid because what you make with it will taste bitter. Some chefs can smell or taste the flour and know. I've had to just toss things out after making them. I store my flour and baked goods in the freezer when I can. This will depend on your setup.

When you don't have much refrigerator space, you might be wondering what needs to be stored in the fridge and what doesn't. Obviously, if you are trying to ripen a fruit such as a tomato or a peach, it's going to need to sit out on the counter. Once you cut into a fruit, like an avocado, pineapple, or apple, anything not eaten right away will need to be put in the fridge, but even fully ripe fruit will last a few more days sitting out.

Garlic, onions, potatoes, and winter squashes can sit out much longer than fruits. I never put ginger and garlic in the fridge at all. As long as you have a cool spot (usually a lower cupboard or shelf) to keep onions, potatoes, and gourds, they can actually stay good for quite a while. Apples also can stay fresh as long as they have a cool, dry environment. Much will depend on the climate you are in, what the air is like inside your camper van, and where you are parked. Figure out what works best for you and your situation.

Tools

Most everything in this book can be made with one pot and one pan. Be sure to have a lid for each. When you are getting set up, you may want to err on the side of having too little and adding what you need as you find

you need it. Or, get everything you think you'll need because getting more tools is going to be too much effort. Here is a list of basics, in no particular order, that I find essential:

- Pot with a lid
- Fry pan with a lid
- Vegetable peeler (Kuhn Rikon is a good one)
- Wooden tongs (you can get away without them, but they are super handy)
- Wooden spoon with a long handle for cooking
- Silverware for at least two people (even if you are the only one)
- Bowl and mug for each person
- Good sharp kitchen knife
- Cutting board
- Can opener
- Kitchen towels (at least two)

Here are more tools that, while not absolutely essential, are really nice to have:

- Measuring cups
- Measuring spoons
- Whisk
- Juice squeezer
- Microplane grater
- Colander
- Sushi mat
- Benriner (a fantastic tool for shredding vegetables—it's basically a small mandolin.)
- Oven mitts
- Bakeware that fits in your oven—if you have one
- Mixing bowl(s)
- Silicon trivet that doubles as a grip

What else you will need is going to depend on how many people you have and what your space situation is like. Make sure you have at least a medium bowl and a mug for each person. Plates are great, but bowls are more versatile. I lived for years with just one bowl, plate, and mug. Part of camping is being resourceful, so assess what your space situation will allow before purchasing too much at once.

The Recipes

CHAPTER 3
Breakfasts

Oat Milk French Toast

Prep Time: 3 minutes
Cooking Time: 5 minutes
Serves: 1

1 egg

½ cup oat milk

2 slices bread (stale bread works best, but use what you have)

1 tablespoon coconut oil

fruit, to serve

maple syrup, to serve

This is probably the simplest French toast recipe. I prefer the Pacific Foods brand of oat milk right now, but there are many good ones out there. This one is naturally sweet with no added sugar, which eliminates the need for any sweetener in the recipe.

1. Whisk the egg and oat milk together.
2. Dip the bread into the mixture and soak thoroughly.
3. Heat the oil in a fry pan.
4. Fry the soaked bread on both sides.
5. Serve with fruit and maple syrup.

Dutch Baby for One

Prep Time: 10 minutes
Cooking Time: 10 minutes
Serves: 1

2 teaspoons Nutiva organic shortening or coconut oil

1 egg

¼ cup Pacific Foods Original Organic Oat milk

splash of vanilla extract

¼ cup all-purpose flour

optional toppings of your choice, such as yogurt, maple syrup, fresh fruit, toasted seeds, and so on

A Dutch baby might seem too fancy for the road—but it's actually a very easy fluffy pancake that you bake, instead of fry, in a pan. With an eggier flavor, it uses far less flour than flapjacks.

1. Preheat the oven to 475°F. Melt the shortening or oil in a small Pyrex pan (or other single-serving pan) by placing the oil in the pan and putting it in the oven for 1 or 2 minutes. Then swirl or use a wooden knife to coat the bottom and sides of the pan.

2. Mix the egg, milk, and vanilla together. Whisk in the flour until smooth, though there might be a few tiny lumps. Don't overmix.

3. Pour the batter into the pan with the hot oil, and then bake for 10 minutes until browned and crisp around the edges and light in the center.

4. If you are taking a photo of this beauty, get all set up before taking it out of the oven because the wonderful puffiness falls fast.

5. Serve with toppings.

Biscuits on the Burner

Prep Time: 8 minutes
Cooking Time: 10 minutes
Serves: 2

1 cup all-purpose flour

1½ teaspoons baking powder

¼ teaspoon sea salt

3 tablespoons Nutiva
shortening or coconut
oil, divided

½ cup oat milk

I like to whip up these fry pan biscuits because they don't take much time and because they are not baked—so they don't heat up my whole home. I prefer these soft rolls with their crisp tops to have less of a baking powder taste; but if you love that, add in a half teaspoon more baking powder than my recipe calls for, and you'll be all set.

1. Combine the flour, baking powder, and sea salt in a mixing bowl.
2. Cut in 2 tablespoons of the shortening or oil with a fork.
3. Mix in the oat milk to form a dough.
4. Divide the dough into 6 pieces.
5. Make flattened rounds out of each piece of dough.
6. Place the remaining 1 tablespoon of shortening or oil in a fry pan over medium-high heat.
7. Put the biscuits into the pan and cover with a lid.
8. Cook for 5 minutes. The side on the pan will be brown.
9. Flip each biscuit and cook for another 5 minutes.
10. Allow the hot biscuits to cool on paper towels for a few minutes before serving.

Baked Frittata

Prep Time: 10 minutes
Cooking Time: 20 minutes
Serves: 1

2+ teaspoons olive oil
(the plus is for oiling
your baking dish)

3 large kale leaves, washed,
trimmed, and chopped

2 large green onions, washed,
trimmed, and chopped

2 to 3 eggs

2 to 3 teaspoons milk of
your choice (I use oat)

salt and pepper to taste

Of course you can do a frittata in a skillet and then stick it under the broiler for the last few minutes, but if you're going to turn on an oven or toaster oven anyway—baking your personal crustless mini quiche is an easy way to go. I used green onions and kale simply because, if you have those in your fridge, you'll want ways to use them all up. Use any combo you like. Most people add cheese but I find I don't need it. As always—make this recipe the way *you* like it.

1. Preheat the oven to 425°F.
2. While the oven heats, put 2 teaspoons of olive oil in a fry pan and sauté the vegetables.
3. Let the vegetables cool so they don't cook the eggs.
4. Crack the eggs into a bowl and whisk in the milk just enough to combine.
5. Add a sprinkle of salt and pepper.
6. Mix in the cooled vegetables.
7. Oil a small baking dish (6-inch round or 4 x 8-inch, etc.).
8. Pour the mixture into the baking dish.
9. Bake for 15 to 17 minutes.
10. Serve.

Simple Hot Cereal

Prep Time: 3 minutes
Cooking Time: 5 to 10 minutes
Serves: 1 to 2

½ cup brown teff flour

1½ cups water

¼ teaspoon cinnamon

raw honey to taste

berries or other sliced
fruit (optional)

oat milk (optional)

Oatmeal might be the only hot cereal you've had experience with, but many different grains make a wonderful morning meal. I learned this trick of making porridge out of whole grain flours for a creamy, sweet breakfast. You could also try it savory like polenta.

1. Place the teff flour in a pot over medium-high heat.

2. Stir continuously.

3. When the flour begins to be fragrant (about 1 or 2 minutes), add the water and continue to stir until you get your desired consistency.

4. Add the cinnamon and honey, then top with fruit, if using. Add oat milk if desired.

CHAPTER 4
Salads

Celery Parsnip Salad

Prep Time: 6 to 10 minutes
Cooking Time: 0 minutes
Serves: 1 to 2

2 parsnips, peeled
and trimmed

2 ribs celery, peeled,
trimmed, and chopped

pinch of sea salt

2 to 3 tablespoons
Vegenaise or mayonnaise

black pepper to taste

Parsnips are such an overlooked vegetable. That might be because they taste best in the cooler seasons when their flavor is sweet like a winter squash. Out of season, parsnips can be bitter or too fibrous to enjoy. Usually I roast them or put them into a cooked dish, but here is one way you can enjoy them raw.

1. Using a grater or a Benriner, shred the parsnips into a bowl.
2. Add the celery and mix in a pinch of sea salt.
3. Stir in the Vegenaise or mayo to taste. (It will depend on how big your parsnips are.)
4. Sprinkle in black pepper and stir.

Burger Salad

Prep Time: 8 minutes
Cooking Time: 10 to 18 minutes
Serves: 1

1 tablespoon olive oil

1 small sweet potato, peeled and cut into bite-sized pieces

sea salt

1 to 2 cups salad greens

1 carrot, peeled and sliced

¼ pound ground beef

2 to 3 pickle slices (optional)

2 to 3 tomato slices (optional)

salad dressing of your choice

Burgers are great in so many forms. The usual way, served on a bun with fries, might not give you quite the same fresh feeling as this salad. I've added fried sweet potatoes into the salad, which makes it a hearty meal that you can cook quickly in a pan.

If you have only one burner, you can do the potatoes and burger in the same skillet.

1. Place the oil in the fry pan over medium heat.

2. Add the potatoes and stir to coat with the oil.

3. Add a sprinkle of sea salt.

4. Stir occasionally to lightly brown all sides and cook the potatoes through.

5. While the potatoes cook, put the greens and carrots on a plate.

6. If you are using one pan, you can put the potatoes on a separate plate to cool if you don't want them to wilt the greens, or go ahead and add them in with the carrots.

7. Form the ground beef into a patty.

8. Put a couple of tablespoons of water into a fry pan over medium heat. The water will bubble.

9. Place the beef patty into the fry pan, to the side of the water if possible.

10. Place a lid on the pan and cook for 4 minutes.

11. Flip the burger and replace the lid. (If there is no water left in the pan, add 1 or 2 tablespoons.)

12. Cook for an additional 4 minutes.

13. Place the burger on the salad, top with pickle slices, if using, and tomato slices, if using and add your favorite dressing.

Super Slaw

Prep Time: 7 minutes
Cooking Time: 0 minutes
Serves: 1

¼ small cabbage, shredded

1 carrot, shredded

1 red radish, shredded

1 tablespoon chopped
fresh parsley

¼ pound sliced turkey
(or protein of choice)

Cider Vinegar Dressing
(page 121), Vegenaise, or
a dressing of your choice

Who says slaw needs to be a side dish? This whole meal salad is great any time you need a quick camper van meal that does not involve turning on a burner. It's good with vegan smoked turkey or regular turkey, or try adding any protein you might have on hand.

1. You can make this salad by shredding all the ingredients in a bowl that you might want to eat out of and thereby save washing an extra dish.

2. Mix all the ingredients together and add Cider Vinegar Dressing, Vegenaise, or a dressing of your choice.

Easy Chicken Salad

Prep Time: 10 minutes
Cooking Time: 10 to 12 minutes
Serves: 1 to 2

1 large boneless, skinless
chicken breast (usually
about ½ pound)

Water for cooking the
chicken and the noodles

Bifun or somen noodles

2 to 3 cups chopped
romaine lettuce

2 to 3 carrots, scrubbed
and chopped

2 to 3 ribs celery,
peeled and sliced

1 teaspoon chopped chives
for garnish (optional)

dressing of your choice

I often make this quick and satisfying salad with leftover chicken, but when someone is coming over, it's also nice if you start from scratch. It's so simple that you can add a dessert and they'll think you're a wizard making five-star lunches from your camper van. Scenery included.

1. Cut off any excess fat on the chicken breast and place the chicken in a pan that has a lid.

2. Add about ½ inch of water and bring the chicken and water to a boil.

3. Turn the heat down to keep a simmer going and let the chicken cook through. For the average ½-pound breast, it will be about 10 minutes. (Check to make sure there is no pink in the middle.)

4. While the chicken cooks, heat a second pot of water for the noodles. (If you don't have a second pot or burner, you can cook the noodles before or after the chicken.)

5. Use the appropriate amount of noodles that you enjoy and cook according to the directions on the package.

6. When the chicken is cooked through, place it on a plate to cool.

7. Assemble the lettuce on one or two plates.

8. Top the lettuce with the carrots and celery.

9. Top that with some noodles.

10. Tear the pieces of chicken apart with your hands and add them to the salad.

11. Sprinkle the chives on top, if using, and add your favorite dressing.

Pickle Salad

Prep Time: 8 minutes
Cooking Time: 1 hour to
overnight
Serves: 2

1 carrot, washed, trimmed,
and sliced thin

1 zucchini, washed,
trimmed, and sliced thin

1 fennel bulb, trimmed
and sliced thin

2 large pinches of sea salt

2 teaspoons olive oil

juice of 1 lemon

This simple salad can be made with a single vegetable, like
fennel, or with several vegetables. The longer it sits, the
more the enzymes of the salt and lemon will break down the
vegetables, so there will be more liquid in the bottom of the
bowl.

1. Place the vegetable slices in a bowl.

2. Sprinkle with the sea salt and stir.

3. Add the olive oil and juice from the lemon. Stir.

4. Place a plate or bowl that fits down on top of the vegetables
   like a press, if you can. Place a heavy jar or can on top of
   that. (If not, just let the vegetables sit with a plate or cotton
   cloth over the bowl.)

5. Allow the salad to sit on the counter for at least 1 hour, up to
   8 hours, before eating or putting it in the fridge or cooler.

Quinoa Kitchen Salad

Prep Time: 8 minutes
Cooking Time: 20 minutes
Serves: 2

½ cup quinoa, sorted
and rinsed

1 cup water

pinch of sea salt

2 to 4 slices grilled or
pan-fried tofu, or your
favorite soft cheese

1 to 2 teaspoons coconut oil

1 shallot, sliced

2 carrots, chopped

5 to 10 pickle slices, cut into
smaller pieces (approximately)

2 tablespoons chopped
fresh parsley

dressing of your choice

2 handfuls of lettuce
or arugula

This is the sort of easy gourmet meal you can customize to whatever you have on hand. The variety of flavors and textures make a satisfying combination that works for lunch or dinner.

1. Place the washed quinoa and water into a pot and bring to a boil.

2. Add a pinch of sea salt.

3. Cover the pot and turn the heat down to low.

4. Simmer for 20 minutes or until all the water has been absorbed.

5. While the quinoa cooks (if you have two burners—if not, cook after the quinoa is done), pan fry your tofu if it is not already grilled (and you are using tofu instead of cheese).

6. Using the same pan as the tofu, fry the shallots in the oil, stirring continuously until brown and crisp.

7. Remove from the heat.

8. Stir the carrots, pickles, and parsley into the quinoa, and then stir in your favorite dressing to taste.

9. Put the lettuce or arugula on a plate, top with half of the quinoa mixture. Place a slice of tofu or cheese on top of the quinoa mixture and top with some of the cooked shallots. Repeat for a second portion.

10. Drizzle your favorite dressing (lemon is a good one) over all.

Tostada Salad

Prep Time: 10 minutes
Cooking Time: 0 minutes
Serves: 1 to 2

5 to 6 large leaves of romaine lettuce, chopped

1 Roma tomato, chopped

½ avocado, cut into chunks

¼ cup cooked corn kernels (frozen roasted corn, or kernels cut from a fresh steamed ear)

¼ (15-ounce) can black bans

2 to 4 tablespoons Cider Vinegar Dressing (or your choice)

½ lemon or lime

This is my favorite tostada salad. You can put a shell at the bottom, break it up into the salad, or leave it out entirely. I usually make this with Cider Vinegar Dressing (page 121), with added lemon or lime.

1. To chop the romaine leaves, stack the leaves and then roll them up into a cigar shape. Next slice the rolled leaves from end to end so that you are shredding the leaves.

2. Place the chopped romaine into a bowl along with the other vegetables and beans.

3. Stir in the dressing and the juice from half of the lemon or lime.

Tofu Stick Salad

Prep Time: 10 minutes
Cooking Time: 25 minutes
Serves: 2

½ block firm tofu, cut into sticks and patted dry

1 cup winter squash (or use sweet potato if you can't find winter squash), peeled and chopped

2 tablespoons olive oil

2 handfuls of salad greens or arugula

1 small fennel bulb, sliced

Miso Dressing (page 123)

Roasting tofu makes it chewy or even crisp, depending on your oven and the brand you have. This is a fun way to use up tofu, since it is simple and easy to do. Blended with all the other flavors in the salad, it doesn't even need to be marinated beforehand.

1. Preheat the oven to 450°F. If your camper van has an oven big enough to roast both the tofu and squash at the same time, toss them together in the olive oil, arrange on a baking sheet lined with parchment paper, and bake for 25 minutes.

2. If not, just put the tofu on a baking tray and coat with 1 tablespoon of the oil, and bake as directed above.

3. Place the other tablespoon of oil in a fry pan.

4. Pan fry the squash until tender and cooked through.

5. Arrange the greens on two plates.

6. Sprinkle fennel slices over the greens.

7. Add the cooked squash and tofu pieces and top with Miso Dressing.

Chickpea Salad in Avocado

Prep Time: 8 to 10 minutes
Cooking Time: 0 minutes
Serves: 2

1 lemon

2 stalks celery, peeled and rinsed

2 tablespoons Vegenaise or mayonnaise

1 cup cooked chickpeas

2 cups salad greens

1 ripe avocado, peeled and halved

Carrot Condiment (page 65)

Buttery avocado is a perfect partner for this easy chickpea salad. The flavors go very well with the lemon dressing. If you have some Carrot Condiment left over from the quesadilla recipe (page 63), it's a nice addition for color and flavor, and you can easily use up your camper van fixings.

1. Juice the lemon and chop the celery.

2. Mix the lemon juice and Vegenaise together to make a dressing.

3. In a bowl, mix the chickpeas with the celery and the lemon-Vegenaise dressing.

4. Place the salad greens on two plates.

5. Place half of the avocado on each plate.

6. Fill the avocado halves with the chickpea mixture and top with the Carrot Condiment.

CHAPTER 5
Soups

Chive Radish Consommé

Prep Time: 3 minutes
Cooking Time: 3 minutes
Serves: 1 to 2

2½ cups water

3 to 5 radishes, sliced

1 tablespoon chopped chives

umeboshi vinegar to taste

This simple clear soup is a refreshing way to start a meal. Radishes are thought to help with digestion and so is umeboshi. This soup is nice hot or cold, plus super fast to make.

1. Place the water in a pan over medium-high heat.

2. Add the radish and chive pieces and bring to a boil.

3. Let it simmer for a minute or so, then turn off the heat.

4. Add the umeboshi vinegar to taste. Start with a ½ teaspoon and then keep adding a dash or two to find the right saltiness for you. Be careful not to put so much ume of the vinegar into the soup that it drowns out the sweetness of the vegetables.

Backwoods Miso Soup with Rice Crisps

Prep Time: 8 minutes
Cooking Time: 10 minutes
Serves: 2

1 tablespoon olive oil

1 large green onion,
washed and chopped

1 stalk celery, peeled
and chopped

1 carrot, chopped

2 to 3 dried shiitake
mushrooms

1 cup shredded cabbage

1 small burdock,
chopped (optional)

1 handful of small greens,
like arugula (optional)

2 to 4 teaspoons miso paste
(you can always add more
miso paste, so start small
and add to your taste)

2 or 3 tablespoons water,
plus more for the soup

3 tablespoons coconut oil

2 to 3 rice wraps
(sometimes called 6-inch
spring roll wraps)

This version of miso soup can be made with anything you have on hand. Use whatever type of miso paste you like. The darker ones, like red or barley miso, will give you an earthy feel. The lighter pastes, such as white miso or chickpea miso, are a little lighter and sweeter.

1. Place the olive oil in a medium pot over medium heat.

2. Add the green onion and stir for 1 minute.

3. Add the other vegetables with enough water to cover the vegetables, then turn the heat to high until the mixture reaches a boil.

4. Turn the heat down and simmer for 7 to 10 minutes.

5. Stir the miso paste into a few tablespoons of water or broth to dissolve and then add to the pot.

6. Remove the pot from the heat.

7. Place the coconut oil in a small fry pan on the burner and let the oil get hot but not smoking.

8. Cut each wrap into four pieces with scissors, making triangular pieces.

9. When the oil is pretty hot, drop in a piece of the rice wrap. It will sizzle and curl up as it puffs. If you don't get white puffs, your oil may not be hot enough.

10. Pull out each piece with tongs.

11. One by one, drop the rice pieces into the oil to make crisps.

12. Serve each bowl of soup with a crisp or two on top.

Friendly French Onion Soup

Prep Time: 5 minutes
Cooking Time: 45 minutes
Serves: 2

1 tablespoon olive or
toasted sesame oil

1 large onion, peeled and
cut into half-moon slices

pinch of dried basil

2 small dried shiitake
mushrooms

2 cups water (approximately)

2 teaspoons organic tamari

The long, slow simmering of onions makes them sweet. You can cook them as long as you want to get them completely caramelized, or just let them melt into a soft pile before adding the other ingredients. For a traditional type of French onion soup, you can always add some cheese and croutons on top, but it really doesn't need it.

1. Place the oil in a pot over medium heat.

2. Add the onion slices and stir to coat with the oil.

3. When the onions are sizzling, place a lid on the pot and turn the heat down to low.

4. Stir occasionally and let the onions simmer for about 35 minutes.

5. Add the dried basil, shiitake mushrooms, and water to completely cover.

6. Stir in the tamari.

7. Simmer for a few minutes to let the flavors meld.

Chickpea Stew

Prep Time: 10 minutes
Cooking Time: 10 minutes
Serves: 1 to 2

1 tablespoon olive oil

¼ onion, chopped

1 medium carrot, sliced

1 large rib celery,
peeled and sliced

1 small burdock,
chopped (optional)

1 cup cooked chickpeas
(approximately)

1 tablespoon chopped
fresh parsley

water to cover

1 to 2 teaspoons white
miso paste, to taste

This is a great recipe to have in a camper van since you can toss everything in a pot, simmer it for 10 minutes, and *voilà*, you have a hearty meal that goes great with any whole grain or bread, such as Biscuits on the Burner (page 31).

1. Place the oil in a pot, over medium heat.
2. Add the onion, carrot, celery, and burdock (if using).
3. Stir for a minute.
4. Add the chickpeas and any of their liquid.
5. Add the parsley.
6. Add water to just cover the ingredients.
7. Bring to a boil and then turn the heat down to simmer for 8 to 10 minutes.
8. Turn off the heat and stir the miso paste in a little bowl with a bit of the broth and then add it to the pot. You may wish to blend part of the soup with an immersion blender to make it even creamier.

CHAPTER 6
Mains

Quesadilla with Carrot Condiment

Prep Time: 8 minutes
Cooking Time: 10 minutes
Serves: 2

2 slices feta type of cheese

2 teaspoons parmesan
type of cheese

2 slices of a mozzarella
type of cheese (or vegan
slices like Follow Your
Heart, Chao, Violife, etc.)

4 to 10 large spinach leaves,
washed and patted dry

2 flour wraps (wheat, spelt,
rice flour, or coconut flour
wraps will all work)

Quesadillas are one of the most simple pleasures. I find that using a nonstick pan makes it easier to get the outsides browned and crisp, but that could be the type of wraps I use. I keep mine in the freezer so when I want to use one, I turn on the heat under the pan and place the wrap in it, flipping once to get both sides defrosted in a minute or two. This recipe uses three cheeses to get a complex flavor, but one is also enough. The spinach is added for flavor and to bring up the nutrients, but it too is an addition that can be left out or swapped for tomato, basil, or anything you might enjoy.

1. Lay half of each cheese and spinach on the bottom half of a wrap.

2. Place the rest of the cheeses and spinach on the bottom half of the second wrap.

3. Fold over the top of each wrap to create two sandwiches that look like semicircles.

4. Place a fry pan over medium heat with nothing in it—no oil or water.

5. If the pan is big enough to hold both sandwiches, put them both in the pan.

6. When the first side is brown, flip and brown the second side.

7. Turn the heat off and put a lid on the pan for an additional 1 or 2 minutes to make sure the cheeses are melted.

8. Remove from the pan and serve with some Carrot Condiment (page 65).

Carrot Condiment

Prep Time: 3 minutes
Cooking Time: 0 minutes
Serves: 1 to 2

1 medium carrot, shredded
on a Microplane grater

⅛ teaspoon sea salt

¼ teaspoon ground cumin

4 to 6 chives, chopped

1 clove garlic, sliced and
minced (optional)

This carrot condiment is better after sitting out for an hour or
more, as the salt starts breaking down the structure and water
is released. But you can also use it right away. Use raw garlic if
you like a spicier taste.

1. Mix all the ingredients in a bowl and leave on the counter for
    1 hour, if possible.

Camper Van Bean Burger

Prep Time: 15 minutes
Cooking Time: 10 minutes
Serves: 2

¾ can of black beans (use
the rest in the Tostada Salad
recipe on page 49)

2 teaspoons olive oil

¼ large red onion, diced

2 stalks celery, peeled,
trimmed, and diced

2 cloves garlic, chopped

2 tablespoons fresh
parsley, chopped

½ teaspoon dried sage

½ teaspoon dried rosemary

½ teaspoon dried thyme

tamari to taste

1 lemon, washed

1 scant teaspoon
prepared mustard

2 to 3 teaspoons
bread crumbs

2 teaspoons arrowroot

2 teaspoons olive
or coconut oil

While this isn't the quickest way to make a burger, it is a great vegan option. You can do this with one fry pan and limited use of propane, so it works equally well in a camper van as it does in any kitchen. If you don't have buns, sliced bread is nice—or put it in a salad.

1. Place the beans in a heat-proof bowl.

2. Place the olive oil in a fry pan over medium heat.

3. Add the onions, celery, garlic, parsley, sage, rosemary, and thyme.

4. Stir until the onions are glossy and cooked through.

5. Add a dash of tamari.

6. Transfer the mixture to the bowl with the beans.

7. Zest a quarter of the lemon's peel into the bowl, and then slice the lemon and squeeze about 2 teaspoons worth of juice into the veggie mix.

8. Stir in the mustard, breadcrumbs, and arrowroot.

9. Taste to adjust the tamari to your liking.

10. Mix well by hand or use a hand blender to make the patties more cohesive.

11. Form about 4 burgers.

12. Place another 2 teaspoons of oil in the fry pan and cook the burgers on each side.

13. You may wish to brown them, but as long as the arrowroot gets heated up, it will hold the patties together.

Turkey Meatballs with Red Pepper Sauce

Prep Time: 10 minutes
Cooking Time: 15 minutes
Serves: 2

4 tablespoons olive oil, divided

1 red bell pepper, sliced

1 clove garlic, sliced

1 tablespoon lemon juice

2 tablespoons oat milk

dash of sea salt

2 green onions, thinly sliced or chopped

2 dashes black pepper

¼ teaspoon black cumin seeds (optional)

½ pound ground turkey

Turkey meatballs can be made all sorts of ways. With burgers, I like adding a little water to the pan to steam the meat, ensuring a moist burger; but with meatballs, I like the outside to brown, at least a little, so I just turn them in the oiled pan. This simple red pepper sauce is a nice addition.

1. Place 1 tablespoon of olive oil into a fry pan over medium-high heat.

2. Cook the bell pepper for about 5 minutes.

3. Turn off the heat, then toss the garlic into the pan.

4. In a blender bowl or other container, add 2 tablespoons of olive oil, lemon juice, and oat milk.

5. Add the cooked pepper slices, garlic, and whatever olive oil is in the pan to the container.

6. Add the sea salt and blend with a blender or hand mixer. Set the sauce aside.

7. Stir the green onions, black pepper, and black cumin seeds, if using, into the ground turkey.

8. Form 8 small meatballs.

9. Add the last tablespoon of olive oil to the pan, over medium heat.

10. Cook the meatballs by browning them on at least two sides and cooking until white all the way through, approximately 6 to 7 minutes.

11. Spoon the red pepper sauce over the meatballs.

Whatcha Got Risotto

Prep Time: 5 minutes
Cooking Time: 45 minutes
Serves: 2

2 teaspoons olive oil

1 clove garlic, chopped

1 shallot, chopped

¾ cup brown rice

1 pinch saffron threads (or herbs of your choice)

2½ to 3 cups broth, divided (any stock or broth will work, but use vegetable or chicken with saffron)

1 cup tofu, cut or torn into bite-sized pieces

2 cups chopped vegetables (1½ cups trimmed and chopped asparagus and ½ cup English peas are pictured)

tamari to taste (optional—use the tamari only if your broth does not contain any salt)

While this is not a fast-cooking dish, it can be a complete and satisfying meal that you make in one pan. I'm using short-grain brown rice instead of Arborio rice, but you could really use any grain you want—go by the cooking time of that grain. And, of course, you can use whatever vegetables you choose. Saffron adds a lovely color and flavor, or you can swap it out for basil, other herbs of your choice, or turmeric.

1. Place the oil in a skillet over medium heat.

2. Add the garlic and shallot and stir for a minute.

3. Add the rice and stir.

4. Add the saffron (or herbs of your choice).

5. Pour in ½ cup of the broth and stir.

6. Add the tofu.

7. Add another ½ cup of broth.

8. Stir.

9. Place a lid on the pan and let simmer for 10 minutes or so.

10. Add more broth and let it simmer for an additional 15 minutes.

11. Stir and add more broth. Keep adding in the broth every 10 or 15 minutes until the rice is soft and to your liking.

12. Add the vegetables and stir, letting them cook until tender.

13. Add the tamari, if using.

14. The rice will seem to absorb more liquid at a certain point, so keep checking and stirring and adding more broth until you get a creamy dish—about 45 minutes for brown rice.

Miso Chicken

Prep Time: 5 minutes
Cooking Time: 15 minutes
Serves: 1 to 2

2 teaspoons olive oil

¼ onion

1 skinless boneless
chicken breast (a large
one can feed 2 people)

water (to cover chicken
and vegetables, and to
dissolve the miso)

1 large stalk broccoli, peeled
and sliced into smaller pieces

3 carrots, cleaned and
sliced in halves or quarters

2 teaspoons white miso paste

½ to 1 teaspoon agave
syrup or other sweetener

Whatever vegetables you have on hand, from bell pepper to zucchini to peas, would work in this recipe. Since we have used broccoli, carrots, and onions in other recipes, here is a way to use up the rest, cooked in a great-tasting sauce.

1. Place the olive oil in a fry pan over medium heat.

2. Add the onions and sauté for a minute.

3. Add the chicken and water to about ½ inch up the side of the pan.

4. Add the rest of the vegetables.

5. Mix the miso paste with a small amount of water to dissolve the paste.

6. Mix the dissolved miso paste water into the pan.

7. Stir in the agave syrup.

8. After 5 or 6 minutes, flip the chicken over and continue cooking until the chicken is cooked through, approximately 6 or 7 minutes more, depending on thickness.

9. Continue cooking until the liquid is reduced to almost nothing. If the chicken hasn't had enough time to cook through at this point, you can add a tiny bit more water, and continue cooking until the water is gone and everything is done.

Lemongrass Fish

Prep Time: 10 minutes
Cooking Time: 15 minutes
Serves: 2

2 red potatoes

1 bulb fennel, trimmed

1 tablespoon coconut oil

sea salt

1 cup oat milk

1 dash ume vinegar

1 stalk lemongrass, cut
into several pieces

2 fish fillets (cod,
snapper, tilapia, etc.)

2 to 4 large kale leaves,
washed and cut into pieces

ginger (optional)

It's rare that I don't put some sort of onion or garlic in a main dish like this, but with all the flavor from the other vegetables, it doesn't need it. Adding a splash of ume vinegar to the oat milk turns it into buttermilk oat milk, which is a great pairing with lemongrass.

1. Slice the potatoes and fennel into ¼-inch slices.

2. Place the coconut oil in a skillet over medium-high heat.

3. Add the potato and fennel slices and coat with oil.

4. Sprinkle in a pinch of sea salt.

5. Stir occasionally and sauté until the vegetables are tender, about 5 minutes.

6. Remove the vegetables and place on 2 plates. It's okay if there are bits stuck to the pan.

7. Add the oat milk, ume vinegar, lemongrass, and fish to the pan.

8. Add the kale and keep the heat where the milk simmers but doesn't froth over.

9. Cook until the fish is done, about 8 to 10 minutes.

10. If using the ginger, grate a bit of it and squeeze the juice over the fish.

11. Put 1 fillet on each plate on top of the vegetables and pour some of the remaining liquid over each serving.

Pilaf Is All You Need

Prep Time: 8 minutes
Cooking Time: 20 minutes
Serves: 1 to 2

2 teaspoons olive oil

1 clove garlic, chopped

½ cup quinoa, sorted
and rinsed

1 cup water

pinch of sea salt

5 to 7 asparagus spears,
trimmed and cut into pieces
(or use greens, broccoli,
or other vegetables)

1 tablespoon fresh parsley

½ lemon

This quinoa pilaf is quick and simple to do, just the thing for busy camper van life. Without any dairy or animal products, this dish can also sit for hours without refrigeration, so it can be a nice one to pack up and eat on a trail. Add cooked beans or nuts to make it even heartier.

1. Place the oil in the bottom of a pot over medium-high heat.
2. Stir in the garlic and quinoa.
3. Add the water. (Use a little extra if the lid doesn't fit and you get a lot of evaporation.)
4. Bring the mixture to a boil, then add a pinch of sea salt and turn the heat down to a simmer.
5. Add the asparagus and place a lid on the pot.
6. Let it simmer for 15 minutes.
7. Stir in most of the parsley and let it cook for another minute or until all the water has been absorbed.
8. Turn the heat off.
9. Grate the lemon rind to get some zest in the pot.
10. Then squeeze in some of the lemon juice.
11. Stir and serve topped with the leftover parsley as a garnish.

Pan-Roasted Garlic and Broccoli Rolls

Prep Time: 3 minutes
Cooking Time: 5 to 8 minutes
Serves: 1 to 2

1 tablespoon olive oil

1 large stalk broccoli,
trimmed, peeled, and
cut into smaller florets

3 to 4 large cloves
garlic, halved

2 sheets sushi nori

1½ cups cooked brown
rice, approximately

ume paste (optional)

cooked chickpeas (optional)

½ avocado, sliced
into 4 pieces

Roasting garlic usually involves turning on an oven and waiting for close to an hour. Pan roasting speeds up the process for a wonderful result that is quick and perfect for making a vegetable roll.

1. Place the oil in a fry pan over medium heat.

2. Add the broccoli pieces and garlic to the fry pan and stir to coat all the vegetable pieces.

3. Put a lid on the pan.

4. Stir every few minutes and turn the vegetables each time.

5. Cook until the garlic has browned and the broccoli is dark with some blackened tops.

6. While the broccoli and garlic roast, lay a sheet of nori on a sushi mat with the shiny side down and the lines going horizontally.

7. Spread some cooked rice evenly over the bottom half of the nori.

8. Spread a thin layer of the ume paste (if using) along the bottom edge of the rice.

9. Put down a line of chickpeas on top of the ume, if using.

10. Put 2 slices of avocado end to end so they fill up a whole line on or above the other ingredients.

11. Place half of the broccoli and garlic in a line just above the avocado.

12. Roll up your sushi roll using the mat.

13. Repeat, using the rest of the roasted filling for a second roll.

14. Slice into pieces by starting in the middle and slicing out to the ends. Serve.

Carrot Onion Rolls

Prep Time: 5 minutes
Cooking Time: 5 to 8 minutes
Serves: 1 to 2

1 tablespoon olive oil

¼ onion, peeled and sliced into similar-sized pieces to the carrots

1 to 2 carrots, washed, trimmed, and sliced into matchstick pieces

tamari

1 to 2 sheets sushi nori

1 cup cooked brown rice

ume paste

½ small avocado

This is a great sushi roll to do when you think you don't have enough groceries to make a sushi roll. While you could easily incorporate other veggies, many people often end up having extra onions and carrots in their pantry, and here is one way to use up those odds and ends so your van life can be economical all the way around. With the tamari inside the roll, you don't even need a dipping sauce.

1. Place the oil over medium heat in a small to medium fry pan.

2. Add the onion and carrot pieces.

3. Stir and add a splash or 2 of tamari.

4. Add water to just come up halfway on the vegetables.

5. Simmer without a lid until the water has completely evaporated, stir occasionally.

6. As the water is eliminated, the sweetness of the carrots and onions will create a coating on the veggies. Stir more at the end to make sure it's on the veggies and not all stuck to the pan.

7. While the carrots and onions cook, lay a sheet of nori on a sushi mat, and cover the bottom half to two-thirds with cooked rice.

8. Spread a thin strip of ume paste along the bottom of the rice.

9. Slice the avocado into 4 strips and lay 2 across the bottom of the rice.

10. Add veggies on top of the avocado and roll up the sushi from the bottom to the top.

11. Spread a little water on the last bit of nori with your fingers, to help it stick if you need to.

12. Slice each roll from the middle out. You will get about 8 pieces.

Cheesy Cauliflower with Crispy Shallots

Prep Time: 5 minutes
Cooking Time: 10 to 15 minutes
Serves: 1 to 2

1 tablespoon plus 1
teaspoon olive oil

2 to 3 cloves garlic,
peeled and sliced

1 small head of cauliflower,
trimmed and chopped
into bite-sized pieces

splash of tamari

2 to 3 tablespoons water

1 to 2 cups dark greens
(spinach, kale, etc.)

3 to 4 slices melting cheese

1 shallot, sliced

This is basically a casserole you can make in a fry pan instead of turning on an oven. You can add any other veggies or proteins you might want to use up, such as chicken or tofu, carrots, and squash; but I like this simple and satisfying cauliflower-and-greens combo. While I use vegan cheeses that are mild, you might enjoy using anything from mozzarella to goat cheese to fontina.

1. Place the tablespoon of olive oil in a fry pan over medium heat.

2. Add the garlic and stir for a few seconds.

3. Add the cauliflower, a splash of tamari, and 2 to 3 tablespoons of water.

4. Simmer with a lid on until the water is almost gone.

5. Add the greens and keep simmering with the lid on for a few minutes to wilt the greens.

6. Add the cheese and turn off the heat.

7. Place the teaspoon of olive oil in another pan over medium heat.

8. Add the shallot slices and stir occasionally until they start to turn brown.

9. Keep stirring until the shallots are cooked and many have turned crispy.

10. Serve the cauliflower with the shallots on top.

Van Life Summer Rolls

Prep Time: 5 minutes
Cooking Time: 5 minutes
Serves: 1 to 2

water (for softening
rice wraps)

4 small Vietnamese
rice wrap sheets

fresh basil leaves

4 slices of feta (vegan
or regular)

1 carrot, washed and cut
into matchstick pieces

1 small zucchini, washed and
cut into matchstick pieces

Simple and delicious, and you can definitely swap ingredients for whatever you have. For example, instead of basil, use mint or dill. Add in slices of bell pepper or snap peas in place of the zucchini. Whatever you choose, just use the freshest produce you can, because that is what tastes best. While terrific plain, feel free to serve with any of your favorite dressings.

1. Heat about 1 inch of water in a fry pan until hot but not boiling.

2. Turn off the heat under the pan.

3. Place 1 rice wrap sheet into the water to soften. (Give it a few seconds.)

4. Carefully put the wrap on a cutting board.

5. Put 1 large or several tiny basil leaves in the middle of the wrap.

6. Put a slice of feta on top of the basil.

7. Put a few carrots and a few zucchini pieces on top of the cheese.

8. Fold in the sides of the wrap to cover the ingredients like a tiny burrito.

9. Repeat softening and filling the wraps until all the filling is used up, to make 4 rolls.

Personal Pizza in a Pan

Prep Time: 40 minutes
Cooking Time: 10 minutes
Serves: 1

1¼ cups all-purpose flour

¼ teaspoon sea salt

¼ teaspoon baking soda

½ teaspoon coconut sugar

1½ teaspoons olive oil

¼ cup plain yogurt (I use coconut yogurt)

½ to 1 teaspoon water

2 tablespoons pizza sauce (or use 1 to 2 tablespoons of olive oil with sprinkles of garlic, oregano, and basil)

2 slices vegan or other cheese such as mozzarella

½ cup chopped or cut pizza toppings (such as onion slices, broccoli pieces, sliced mushrooms, etc.)

This pizza is so quick and simple to make that it can be faster than ordering takeout! It's not going to rival a brick oven or baking stone pizza, but it is a nice one you can do yourself without yeast or turning on an oven.

1. Mix the flour, salt, baking soda, and coconut sugar in a large bowl.

2. Add the olive oil and yogurt and mix.

3. Using your hands, knead the dough. If it's tough or won't come together, add the water a little at a time and continue to knead into a smooth dough.

4. Let the dough sit in the bowl (preferably in a sunny spot) for a ½ hour or longer. If the weather is cold, you may want it to sit for a few hours, but usually a ½ hour is plenty.

5. Roll out or just pull the dough to form a 7- to 8-inch round.

6. Place the ¼-inch-thick round disk of dough in a fry pan over medium to medium-low heat.

7. Use a fork to prick the dough a bit and then put pizza sauce (or use olive oil, garlic, oregano, and basil) on top, cheese on top of that, and then your favorite toppings.

8. Place a lid on the pan.

9. Cook for about 8 to 10 minutes.

10. The cheese should be melted and the crust will be brown on the bottom. The longer it cooks, the crispier that bottom will get.

Your Fried Rice

Prep Time: 15 minutes

Cooking Time: 10 minutes
Serves: 1

1½ tablespoons oil (if you have toasted sesame oil great; otherwise, use olive oil or coconut oil)

2 green onions, trimmed and sliced thin

1 clove garlic, chopped

1 to 2 carrots, washed, trimmed, and sliced or chopped

1 to 2 ribs celery, sliced

3 small kale leaves, chopped

½ cup thinly sliced cabbage

⅔ cup tofu (any type)

1 tablespoon tamari

2 tablespoons water

1 cup cooked rice

ginger to taste

This is *your* fried rice because whatever veggies you currently have in your camper van, along with some cooked rice, can be used to make a delicious fried rice meal. It doesn't need to be exactly like a restaurant's. It can be your personal creation. This is a basic recipe to spring off from. The ginger is added at the end for maximum benefits and so you can add more or less. But if you love spicy ginger, you can also add some fresh chopped ginger with the veggies.

1. Place the oil in a fry pan over medium-high heat.
2. Add the vegetables and stir to coat with the oil for 1 or 2 minutes.
3. Crumble in the tofu.
4. Sprinkle in the tamari.
5. Depending on your pan, or for softer cooked veggies, add 2 tablespoons of water and simmer for 5 minutes or until the water has reduced by half.
6. Add in the rice and stir for 1 or 2 minutes until the liquid is completely absorbed.
7. Grate the ginger on a Microplane grater to get a dime-sized ball of gratings, and then squeeze the juice into your fried rice and stir. That's it.

CHAPTER 7
Desserts

Honey-Mint Avocado Pudding

Prep Time: 3 minutes
Cooking Time: 3 minutes
Serves: 2

¾ to 1 cup blended avocado

3 tablespoons honey

2 teaspoons peppermint
oil or flavoring

1 tablespoon oat
milk (optional)

½ teaspoon cocoa
powder (optional)

1. Blend the avocado, honey, and peppermint oil together to form a smooth cream.

2. Blend in the oat milk, if using, to get your desired consistency.

3. Serve in bowls, and sprinkle the top with cocoa powder, if using.

Coconut Cream with Caramel Sauce

Prep Time: 5 minutes
Cooking Time: 15 to 20 minutes
Serves: 2 to 3

For the caramel sauce:

½ cup oat milk

½ cup brown rice syrup

½ cup agave syrup
or barley malt

1 teaspoon vanilla extract

2 teaspoons lemon juice

For the coconut cream:

1 can organic coconut
cream, chilled

2 teaspoons vanilla extract

⅓ cup coconut palm sugar

Coconut creams are somewhere between an alternative to ice cream or a whipped topping. You could use this as a frosting or layer it with fruit for a parfait. It's a reason to get a hand blender with a whisk attachment; but it still works, even if all you have is a fork to do the mixing (with a lot of arm strength). You won't get as much air into the mix, but you will still have a creamy treat to enjoy. If you love a strong, sweet taste, feel free to increase the coconut sugar to a ½ cup. If you prefer less sweetness, take it down to a ¼ cup or omit the sugar all together.

1. To make the caramel sauce: Place the oat milk, rice syrup, agave syrup or barley malt, and 1 teaspoon vanilla extract in a pot.

2. Bring the mixture to a boil and then turn the heat down to simmer.

3. Let the mixture cook down to thicken for about 15 to 20 minutes.

4. Then turn off the heat and add the lemon juice. Use hot or cool.

5. To make the coconut cream: While the caramel sauce cooks, put the coconut cream solids into a bowl. Reserve the liquid for the Lemongrass Fish recipe (page 75), or use in your morning cereal, a smoothie, or another recipe.

6. Add the vanilla and coconut palm sugar, then blend well.
   If you have an electric mixer, you will be able to get the
   smoothest consistency; just keep blending and increase the
   speed to get more air into the mixture. If you are using a
   whisk by hand (or fork), just whisk as best you can. It won't
   be perfect and that is okay. Blend all the ingredients well.
   Serve topped with caramel sauce.

Strawberry Cookie Dough Oat Bars

Prep Time: 15 minutes
Cooking Time: 25 minutes
Serves: 4 to 8

½ cup oat flakes

2 cups oat flour

pinch of sea salt

½ cup raw agave syrup

½ cup safflower oil

1 teaspoon vanilla extract

½ cup fresh strawberries

This recipe is wonderfully versatile. Try it with chocolate chips mixed in instead of the strawberries on top, or swirl in your favorite jam. Different oils and sweeteners will yield a different result. This combination made solely with oats makes for a soft bar that might remind you of cookie dough.

1. Preheat the oven to 350°F.

2. Line an 8-inch baking dish with parchment paper.

3. Mix the dry ingredients in a mixing bowl.

4. Mix the agave syrup, oil, and vanilla in another bowl and then add it to the dry ingredients.

5. Mix just until all the dry ingredients are blended in.

6. Pour the batter into the lined pan.

7. Place the strawberries on top.

8. Bake for approximately 25 minutes. The edges will brown and pull away from the pan slightly.

Strawberry Coconut Cream

Prep Time: 5 minutes
Cooking Time: 10 minutes
Serves: 2 to 3

1 can organic coconut cream, chilled

1 teaspoon vanilla extract

⅓ cup coconut palm sugar

½ cup chopped fresh strawberries

This is another variation on the coconut cream theme. Yes, it could be most any common fruit that you like. Strawberries happen to work well with the vanilla-coconut base. Even people who dislike coconut have enjoyed this simple treat.

1. Put the coconut cream solids into a bowl and reserve the liquid for the Lemongrass Fish recipe (page 75), or use in your morning cereal, a smoothie, or another recipe.

2. Add the vanilla and coconut palm sugar, then blend well. If you have an electric mixer, you will be able to get the smoothest consistency—just keep blending and increase the speed to get more air into the mixture. If you are using a whisk by hand (or fork), just whisk as best you can. It won't be perfect and that is okay. Blend all the ingredients well.

3. Fold or blend in the strawberry pieces and serve.

Van Life Seed Brittle

Prep Time: 3 minutes
Cooking Time: 6 to 8 minutes
Serves: 2+

1 cup raw pumpkin seeds

1 cup raw sunflower seeds

pinch of sea salt

1 cup liquid sweetener (½ cup rice syrup and ½ cup maple syrup is a nice blend)

This is a super-simple recipe for a dessert, snack, or breakfast where you don't have to worry about having a candy thermometer or measuring exactly. It's a pour-and-stir type of thing that is a nice way to create a crunchy, sweet treat. Use the measurements as guides. You can try more or less of the ingredients, or add your own favorites, like toasted oats, dried fruits, or cereal.

1. Place the seeds in a fry pan and stir continuously over high heat.

2. Add a pinch of sea salt.

3. When the seeds begin to brown and make popping sounds, keep stirring and add in the syrup(s), which will immediately boil.

4. Stir for 1 or 2 minutes more as the syrup thickens to a hard coating.

5. Spread the hot mixture onto waxed paper or parchment paper, or a large plate.

6. Let it cool and then break into pieces.

Single-Serving Apple Crisp

Prep Time: 5 minutes
Cooking Time: 20 minutes
Serves: 1

1 apple, cored and
cut into chunks

¼ cup water (plus a little
for mixing with arrowroot)

pinch of cinnamon

dash of coconut
sugar (optional)

1 tablespoon Nutiva
shortening

2 tablespoons coconut sugar

couple of drops of
vanilla extract

small pinch of sea salt

1 to 2 tablespoons oat flour

heaping ½ teaspoon of
arrowroot (or kudzu powder)

I often make this dessert by putting the apples, cinnamon, and arrowroot into a parchment packet and baking it in the oven for 45 minutes, then adding the topping and baking for 10 minutes more. I came up with this version, half in a pot and half in an oven, to cut the oven time down to use less fuel.

1. Preheat your oven or toaster oven to 350°F.

2. Place the apple chunks, water, and cinnamon, and a dash of coconut sugar (if using), in a pot over medium heat.

3. Simmer for 5 to 8 minutes until the apples are tender.

4. While the apples cook, mix the shortening, coconut sugar, vanilla, and salt in a cup or small bowl.

5. Mix in the flour to make a dough.

6. Mix the arrowroot (or kudzu) with a small amount of water and mix into the apples. It will immediately form the glaze/filling.

7. Transfer the hot apple mixture to a heatproof baking dish and crumble the dough on top.

8. Bake in the oven for 10 minutes or until the topping is brown.

Simple Fruit Gel

Prep Time: 0 to 3 minutes
Cooking Time: 5 to 10 minutes
Serves: 2 to 3

1 basket fresh or 12 ounces frozen blueberries

1 apple, cored and cut into chunks

¼ cup water (or apple or pear juice, if desired)

1½ teaspoons agar powder

½ teaspoon cinnamon

⅓ cup coconut sugar

¼ lemon, seeds removed

Fruit gels can be made creamy or firm. This one is in the middle because lemon keeps the agar from being too solid. If you want to ensure a creamy fruit gel, mix in a little diluted kudzu at the end of cooking. To make them year-round, you can pick up a bag of frozen fruit and use it frozen or defrosted. For extra flavor or sweetness, you can substitute apple or pear juice in place of the water.

1. Place the fruit and water (or juice) into a saucepan over medium heat.

2. Add the agar and stir. Depending on your pot, you may need to add a bit more water.

3. Let the mixture come to a boil and then turn the heat down to just keep the simmer going.

4. Add the cinnamon and coconut sugar.

5. Turn off the heat and squeeze in the juice from the lemon.

6. Let cool.

CHAPTER 8
Drinks and Snacks

Instant Lemonade

Prep Time: 5 minutes
Cooking Time: 0 minutes
Serves: 1 to 2

4 lemons

2 cups water

¼ cup raw agave syrup

If you think making lemonade involves hours of squeezing lemons for a big pitcher—think smaller. Lemonade for one or two people is quick and delicious. I use agave as the sweetener because it doesn't add a strong taste like maple syrup or coconut sugar does—but use your favorite sweetener. A cool glass of lemonade always makes a simple lunch more of a treat.

1. Squeeze the juice of the lemons into a container.
2. Add the water and agave syrup.
3. Stir well.

Surprising Blueberry Soda Water

Prep Time: 0 minutes
Cooking Time: overnight
Serves: 2

20 fresh blueberries

12 ounces sparkling
or flat water

Water infusions are most likely an ancient thing. Adding fruits, spices, or herbs to water is a lovely way to create refreshing variety. The Brazilian restaurant Woodspoon introduced me to cinnamon stick water. The first time I tried blueberry water, I was surprised by how much I liked it. Allowing the ingredients time to meld will yield more flavor to the water.

1. If you want a stronger flavor, muddle the blueberries a bit by partially crushing them in the water. If you are using frozen berries, you'll want to just plop them in. If using sparkling water, be sure to seal the lid tight.

2. Place the water in your fridge, cooler, or cold stream overnight and enjoy the next day.

Strawberry Oat Milk

Prep Time: 5 minutes
Cooking Time: 2 minutes
Serves: 2

7 fresh strawberries

2 cups oat milk

Every brand of oat milk is going to taste a little different, so your results will rely on that. (I'm using the Pacific Foods brand.) This oat-based beverage is both filling and refreshing. It's so simple, but you can adjust it to your own taste by adding sweetener or vanilla if you wish. The best thing is to have ripe berries that are full of flavor.

1. Rinse the berries and pat dry.
2. Cut off the stem parts and slice the berries in half.
3. Place the berries and oat milk into a tall container.
4. Blend with a hand blender.

Hot Turmeric Oat Milk

Prep Time: 5 minutes
Cooking Time: 5 minutes
Serves: 2

2 cups oat milk

1 teaspoon coconut oil

¼ teaspoon turmeric

dash of black pepper

dash of ground
cardamom (optional)

1 teaspoon honey (optional)

This cozy nourishing drink can be enjoyed hot or cold. Cold is nice, but warm is something like sipping a comforting treat, much like wrapping yourself in a warm blanket on a cold night. Plus, it's touted to have wonderful health benefits.

1. Place all the ingredients, minus the honey (if using), in a saucepan over medium heat.

2. Stir occasionally as the coconut oil melts and the beverage comes to a boil.

3. Turn off the heat and stir in the honey, if using.

4. **Pour** into 2 cups and enjoy.

Flaxseed Tea

Prep Time: 5 minutes
Wait Time: 1 to 8 hours
Serves: 2

about 7 dates or prunes

2 tablespoons whole flaxseeds

3 to 4 cups water

Flaxseeds are wonderfully versatile. You can sprinkle them into salads or cereals for extra crunch or whip them up with water to use in place of eggs in some recipes. Here they impart their flavor, and some texture, to this easy tea/infusion. The dates or prunes add sweetness.

1. Chop the fruit into pieces and put in a container or jar with the other ingredients. Let the mixture sit on the counter for 1 hour and then put it in the cooler or fridge. Stir before serving to meld the flavors.

Camper Van Snacking Seeds

Prep Time: 1 minute
Cooking Time: 5 minutes
Serves: 4

1 cup of raw pumpkin or
sunflower seeds, shelled

tamari or ume vinegar to taste

Fresh roasted seeds can be addictive, so make as many or as few as you like. They are nice to have on hand to sprinkle on top of cereal or veggies, or as a fast snack.

1. Place the seeds in a dry fry pan over medium-high heat.
2. Stir continuously until the seeds begin to turn brown. Pumpkin seeds will start to pop.
3. Turn off the heat and sprinkle in a few drops of tamari or ume vinegar. (You can always add more but you can't take any out, so start with a few drops and adjust as needed.)
4. Stir to coat the seeds.
5. Taste and add a few more drops if needed.
6. Let cool completely before storing the seeds in a jar or bag.

Van Life Pickles

Prep Time: 10 minutes
Curing Time: 8 hours
Serves: about 10

5 to 7 small Persian cucumbers

½ teaspoon sea salt

2 heaping teaspoons coconut sugar

1 tablespoon fenugreek seeds (optional)

6 tablespoons apple cider vinegar

Pickles help digestion and can be a fun addition to any meal. You can use any glass jar and virtually any vegetable. I often pickle the rest of the radishes in a bunch when I've needed only a few for another recipe, but Persian cucumbers are what I use most. I refrigerate my homemade pickles, but I've known people who live in buses, vans, and boats who simply have a jar sitting on a little shelf (often roped in so it won't fall), and use them up quickly. You don't really need to measure when you make pickles, so please use this just as a guide.

1. Slice off the stem end of each cucumber. Rub the end quickly around in a circular fashion on top of the cucumber it was just cut from. This will create a foam that brings the acid up and out of the vegetable.

2. Wash off the foam.

3. Slice off the bottom end of each cucumber, then slice into ¼-inch pieces.

4. Place the cucumber pieces in a bowl and mix well with the salt.

5. Add the coconut sugar, fenugreek (if using), and vinegar. Mix well.

6. Place a plate that fits inside the bowl on top of the vegetables and weigh it down with something. I usually use a jar of honey.

7. Let the pickles sit in the bowl, on a counter overnight or all day, before putting them in a jar in the fridge/cooler.

CHAPTER 9
Dressings

Lemon Shallot Dressing

Prep Time: 5 minutes
Cooking Time: 0 minutes
Serves: 1 to 2

2 tablespoons olive oil

1 teaspoon shallot, chopped fine

1 tablespoon lemon juice

¼ teaspoon agave

salt

pepper

I could also call this lemonade dressing, as it's slightly sweet and lemony, with a tang from the shallots.

1. Place the oil, shallot, lemon juice, and agave in a small bowl.
2. Add a pinch of salt and a dash of pepper.
3. Stir well.

Strawberry Tofu Dressing

Cider Vinegar Dressing

Orange Ginger Basil Dressing

Cider Vinegar Dressing

Prep Time: 3 minutes
Cooking Time: 0 minutes
Serves: 2

2 tablespoons olive oil

2 teaspoons apple
cider vinegar

½ teaspoon umeboshi vinegar

½ teaspoon agave

This is my "go-to" dressing that I whip up often. I've doubled it here for two servings, but you might need more or less. The umeboshi vinegar is the salt in this recipe, so no added salt is needed.

1. Whisk all the ingredients together with a tiny whisk or a fork.

Strawberry Tofu Dressing

Prep Time: 7 minutes
Cooking Time: 2 minutes
Serves: 2+

½ cake (7 ounces)
regular or firm tofu

½ cup strawberries,
trimmed and sliced in half

1 tablespoon olive oil

1 tablespoon apple
cider vinegar

1 tablespoon raw honey

pinch of sea salt

Since the base of this dressing is tofu, it can be a filling dressing compared to others. It works equally well on fruit salads and green salads. The only thing I would never pair it with is beans, since fruit and beans can be a difficult combination to digest. If you want a creamy bean salad dressing, omit the strawberries.

1. Using any type of blender, blend all the ingredients together until smooth.

Orange Ginger Basil Dressing

Prep Time: 5 minutes
Cooking Time: 0 minutes
Serves: about 2

¼ teaspoon ginger juice
from fresh ginger

2 tablespoons olive oil

2 tablespoons fresh
orange juice

½ teaspoon brown
rice vinegar

½ teaspoon fresh
basil, chopped fine

salt and pepper to taste

My friend wanted this dressing on a chicken salad, so I whipped it up for her in a couple of minutes and she was delighted. Basil being in the mint family, I later found this dressing also works with mint.

1. To get ginger juice, simply rub a piece of fresh ginger on a Microplane grater a few times, and grab up the gratings from the back and squeeze the juice that comes out into your dressing. The freshest ginger will have the most juice.

2. Mix all the ingredients well with a small whisk or a fork.

Miso Dressing

Prep Time: 3 minutes
Cooking Time: 0 minutes
Serves: 2

2 tablespoons olive oil

1 tablespoon brown
rice vinegar

1 teaspoon agave

1 teaspoon white miso paste

dash of black pepper

This dressing is both sweet and savory, and adds a lot of flavor. These measurements are all approximate—because you really do not need to get out measuring spoons to make it!

1. Mix all ingredients well before serving.

Avocado Dressing with Fresh Herbs

Prep Time: 7 minutes
Cooking Time: 0 minutes
Serves: 2

1 small ripe avocado

1 tablespoon apple
cider vinegar

¼ teaspoon umeboshi
vinegar (or a pinch of salt)

½ teaspoon fresh herbs,
chopped fine (basil and
chives are what I use)

1 to 2 tablespoons oat
milk (optional)

Avocados are wonderfully versatile. They can be the protein in a salad or sandwich or the base of a dessert, or blended into a smooth pourable sauce. This dressing can be a fun addition to an open-faced sandwich since it won't slide off the way other dressings do.

1. Blend all the ingredients until smooth.
2. If your avocado is not soft enough to blend easily, add a small amount of oat milk and the dressing will thin out as you blend it.

Conversions

Volume

U.S.	U.S. EQUIVALENT	METRIC
1 tablespoon (3 teaspoons)	½ fluid ounce	15 milliliters
¼ cup	2 fluid ounces	60 milliliters
⅓ cup	3 fluid ounces	80 milliliters
½ cup	4 fluid ounces	120 milliliters
⅔ cup	5 fluid ounces	160 milliliters
¾ cup	6 fluid ounces	180 milliliters
1 cup	8 fluid ounces	240 milliliters
2 cups	16 fluid ounces	480 milliliters

Weight

U.S.	METRIC
½ ounce	15 grams
1 ounce	30 grams
2 ounces	60 grams
¼ pound	115 grams
⅓ pound	150 grams
½ pound	225 grams
¾ pound	340 grams
1 pound	450 grams

Temperature

FAHRENHEIT (°F)	CELSIUS (°C)
70°F	20°C
100°F	40°C
120°F	50°C
130°F	55°C
140°F	60°C
150°F	65°C
160°F	70°C
170°F	75°C
180°F	80°C
190°F	90°C
200°F	95°C
220°F	105°C

FAHRENHEIT (°F)	CELSIUS (°C)
240°F	115°C
260°F	125°C
280°F	140°C
300°F	150°C
325°F	165°C
350°F	175°C
375°F	190°C
400°F	200°C
425°F	220°C
450°F	230°C
500°F	260°C

About the Author

Susan Marque is a writer and actor. She holds an MFA in creative writing from The New School and currently lives in Los Angeles.